Pebble Plus

Exploring Space

Constellations

by Martha E. H. Rustad

Consulting Editor: Gail Saunders-Smith, PhD

Consultant: Ilia Iankov Roussev, PhD
Associate Astronomer & Associate Professor
Institute for Astronomy, University of Hawaii at Manoa

CAPSTONE PRESS
a capstone imprint

Pebble Plus is published by Capstone Press,
1710 Roe Crest Drive, North Mankato, Minnesota 56003.
www.capstonepub.com

 Books published by Capstone Press are manufactured with paper
containing at least 10 percent post-consumer waste.

Library of Congress Cataloging-in-Publication Data
Rustad, Martha E. H. (Martha Elizabeth Hillman), 1975–
  Constellations / by Martha E. H. Rustad.
    p. cm.—(Pebble plus. Exploring space)
  Includes bibliographical references and index.
  Summary: "Full-color photographs and simple text provide a brief introduction to various constellations"—Provided by
publisher.
  ISBN 978-1-4296-7582-6 (library binding)
  ISBN 978-1-4296-7892-6 (paperback)
  1. Constellations—Juvenile literature. I. Title.
  QB802.R87 2012
  523.8—dc23   2011021644

Editorial Credits
Erika L. Shores, editor; Alison Thiele, designer; Kathy McColley, production specialist

Photo Credits
Alamy/B.A.E. Inc., 5; World History Archive, 7
Capstone Studio/Karon Dubke, 21
Dreamstime/Igor Sokalski, (star fields) cover, 1, 9, 13, 15 (both), 17, 19
Photo Researchers, Inc/Eckhard Slawik, (star field) 11
Shutterstock/Roman Sotola, (drawing) 17
Space Telescope Science Institute and U.S. Naval Observatory, (drawings) 1, 9, 11, 13, 15 (both), 19

Artistic Effects
Shutterstock: glossygirl21, Primož Cigler, SmallAtomWorks

Note to Parents and Teachers

The Exploring Space series supports national science standards related to earth science. This
book describes and illustrates constellations. The images support early readers in understanding
the text. The repetition of words and phrases helps early readers learn new words. This book
also introduces early readers to subject-specific vocabulary words, which are defined in the
Glossary section. Early readers may need assistance to read some words and to use the Table
of Contents, Glossary, Read More, Internet Sites, and Index sections of the book.

Printed in the United States of America in North Mankato, Minnesota.
102011   006405CGS12

Table of Contents

What Is a Constellation?

Stars twinkle and shine

in the night sky.

Connect the bright dots.

Do you see any patterns?

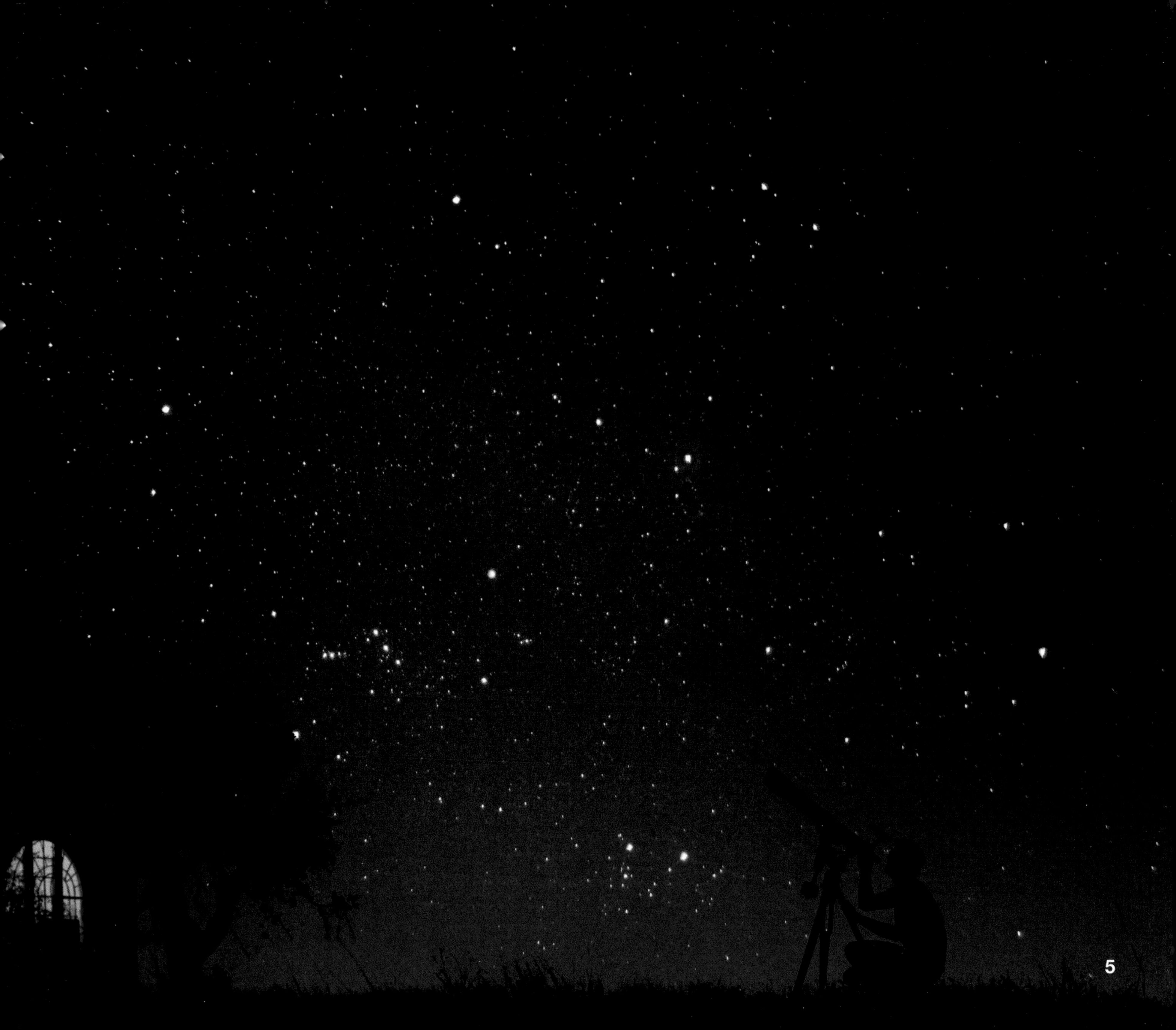

Long ago, people grouped stars

into patterns called constellations.

They named the constellations

and told stories about them.

Today, there are 88 constellations.

7

Famous Constellations

Ursa Minor means "little bear."
It is also called the Little Dipper.
The North Star, or Polaris,
is at one end. This bright star
always points north.

 **How to say it:**

Ursa Minor (ER-suh MY-nur)

Polaris (po-LAHR-iss)

North Star

Ursa Major means "big bear."

Seven stars in its tail

and body form the Big Dipper.

Astronomers use the Big Dipper

to find the North Star.

How to say it:

Ursa Major (ER-suh MAY-jur)

Orion looks like a hunter.

Three bright stars

make Orion's belt.

How to say it:

Orion (oh-RY-uhn)

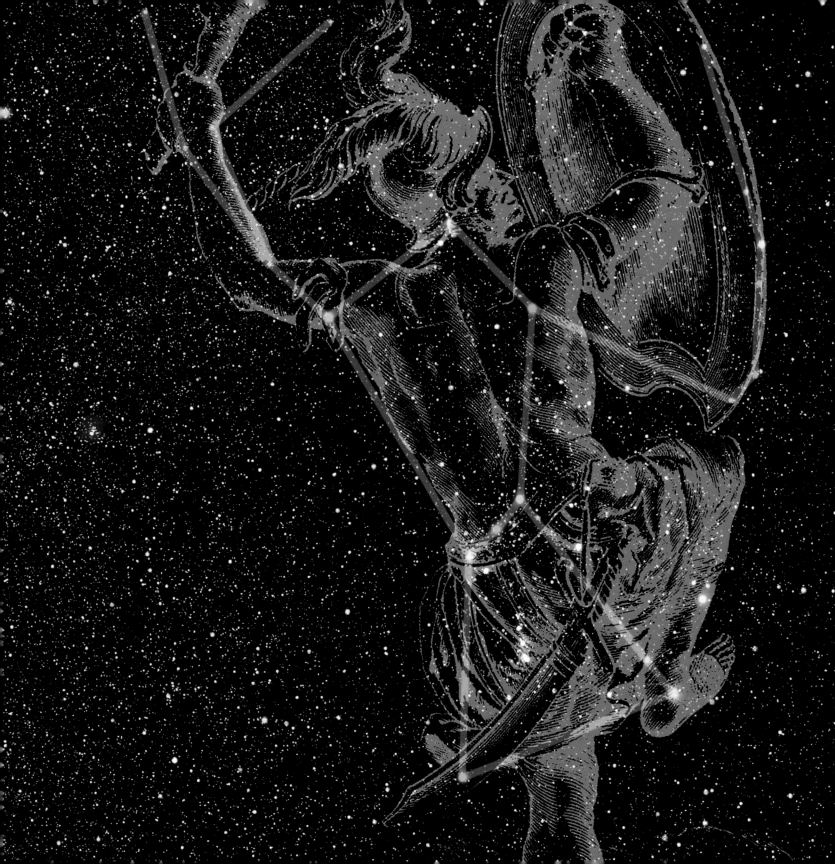

Cassiopeia looks like
the letter W. These five stars
show a queen seated on a throne.
Andromeda is her daughter.

 **How to say it:**

Cassiopeia (CASS-ee-oh-PEE-uh)

Andromeda (an-DRAH-mih-duh)

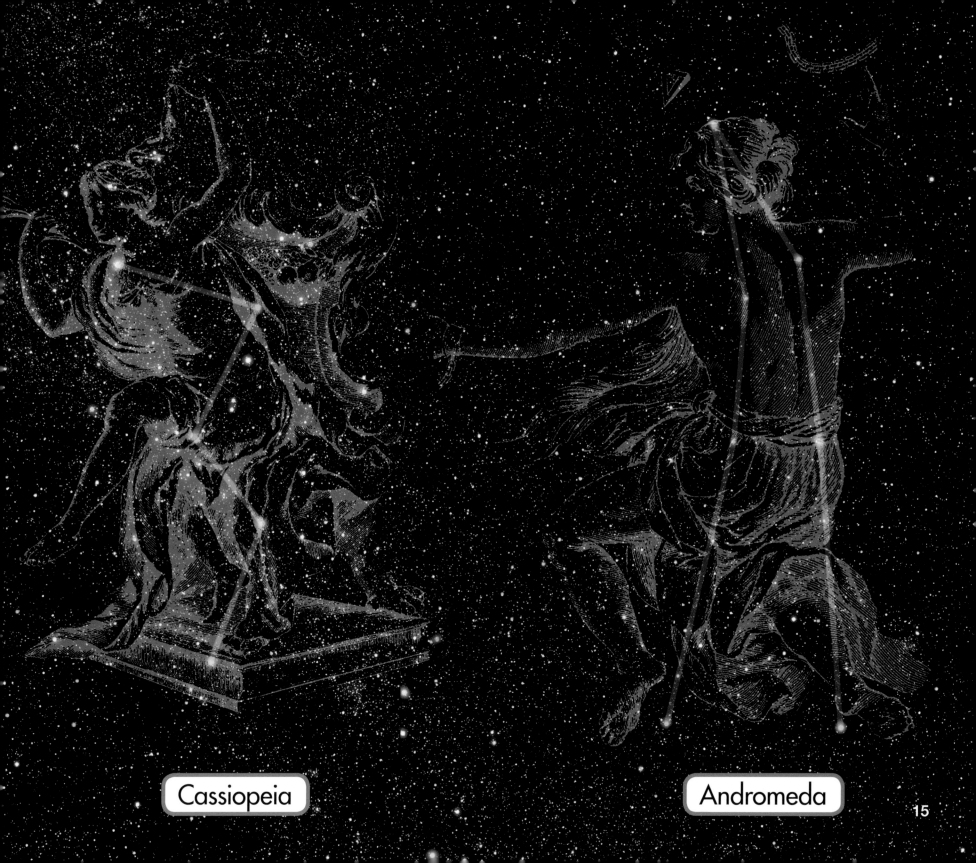

Cassiopeia

Andromeda

Crux is also called

the Southern Cross.

People south of

the equator can see it.

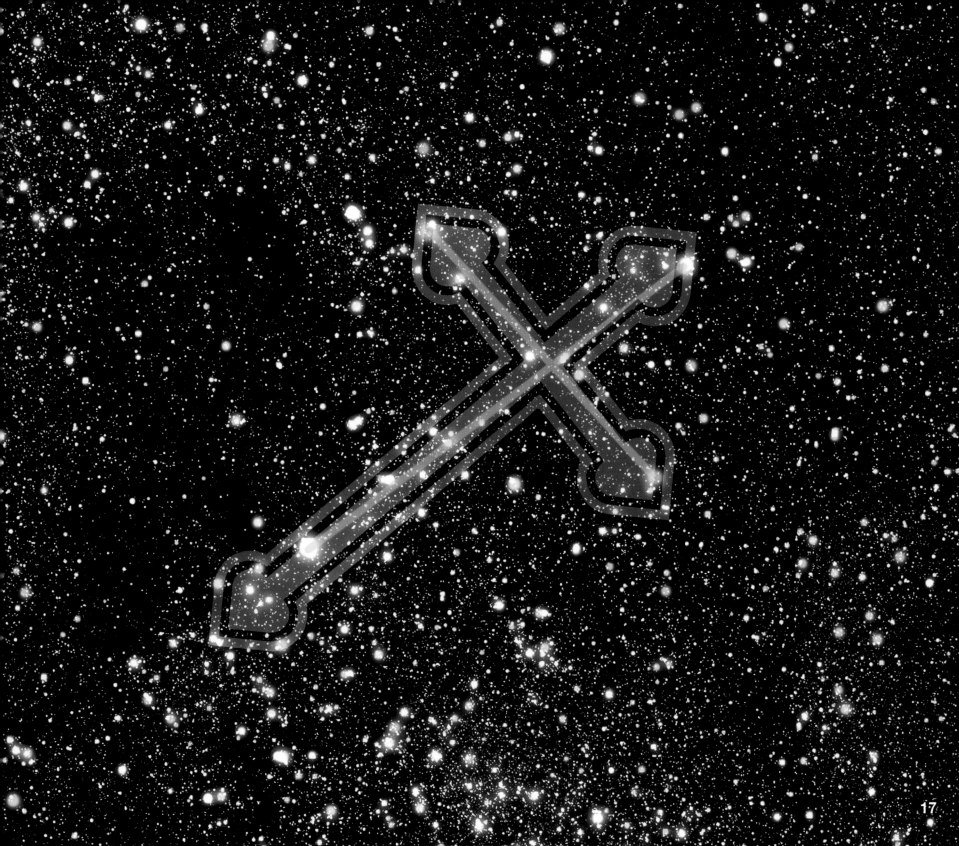

The zodiac is a line
of 13 constellations.
They circle Earth
during the year. We can
see five or six at a time.

Leo is a constellation in the zodiac. Leo means "lion."

Finding Constellations

Earth is always moving in space.
As Earth moves, our view of
the stars changes. Maps of the sky
called star charts help people
find constellations.

Glossary

astronomer—a scientist who studies stars, planets, and other objects in space

equator—an imaginary line around the middle of Earth

star—a ball of hot, bright gases in space

star chart—a map that shows where you can find constellations at different times of night and throughout the year

zodiac—a circular, imaginary belt in the sky that includes the path of the Sun, the moon, and planets; 13 constellations are part of the zodiac

Read More

Goldsworthy, Steve. *Constellations.* Space Science. New York: Weigl Publishers, 2011.

Kim, F. S. *Constellations.* A True Book. New York: Children's Press, 2010.

Zappa, Marcia. *Constellations.* The Universe. Edina, Minn.: ABDO Pub., 2011.

Internet Sites

FactHound offers a safe, fun way to find Internet sites related to this book. All of the sites on FactHound have been researched by our staff.

Here's all you do:

Visit *www.facthound.com*

Type in this code: 9781429675826

Super-cool stuff! Check out projects, games and lots more at **www.capstonekids.com**

Index

Word Count: 188
Grade: 1
Early-Intervention Level: 22